£1·50

RED MEAT
COOK BOOK

Quality Meat Scotland
The Rural Centre – West Mains, Ingliston, Newbridge, EH28 8NZ, Scotland, UK
Tel: +44 (0)131 472 4040   Fax: +44 (0)131 472 4038
Email: info@qmscotland.co.uk Web: www.qmscotland.co.uk
Red Meat Cook Book
Published by Quality Meat Scotland, 2011

ISBN: 978-0-9570709-0-5

Advised retail price: £12.99

CUTS OF MEAT

COOKING MEAT

RECIPES

STEP BY STEP

specially selected

SCOTCH BEEF

PER KI

MINCE 5·7
BRAISING STEAK 6·4
RUMP STEAK 14·8
ENTRECOTE STEAK 27·8
ET STEAK 36·5
10·5

2

Introduction

If you like eating and cooking red meat, specifically beef, lamb and pork, then this book is for you.

Discover what makes Scotch Beef, Scotch Lamb and Specially Selected Pork so special and learn some useful cooking information about red meat, then try some delicious recipes. If you're not confident preparing pork, starting a casserole or carving lamb, follow the three step-by-step methods to help you gain confidence and become the talk of the dinner table!

Red meat can play an important role in the diet as it contains iron, zinc and B vitamins. The iron found in meat is absorbed well by the body and meat has the extra advantage of helping with the absorption of iron from vegetables and cereals. Lean red meat is relatively low in fat and rich in zinc which is needed to help wound healing and for fertility.

Choose the freshest and best quality produce you can for optimum flavour, a well-stocked store cupboard and good simple utensils make cooking much easier too. Herbs used sparingly enhance meat dishes and contribute to colour, taste and aroma. You will discover more as you go through the book.

This book has been produced by Quality Meat Scotland (QMS), the public body responsible for helping the Scottish red meat sector promote Scotch Beef, Scotch Lamb and Specially Selected Pork globally, whilst maintaining the highest standards in Scotland's red meat industry. These standards relate largely to animal welfare and food safety and are some of the strictest in the world. When you see the Scotch Beef, Scotch Lamb and Specially Selected Pork labels in your supermarket, butcher's shop, or restaurant, it's your guarantee that the meat you're buying conforms to QMS standards.

{ World renowned reputation,
great quality of life,
great quality of taste. }

QUALITY AND LABELLING

The focus on animal health and welfare has increased in recent years as people become more educated on the methods involved in meat production.

Quality Meat Scotland has assurance schemes which cover more than 90% of livestock farmed for meat in Scotland. These assurance schemes give consumers the legal guarantee that the meat they buy has come from animals that have spent their whole lives in Scotland being raised to some of the world's strictest standards.

Labelling is becoming increasingly important as it can provide a guarantee on production methods and full product traceability (from farm to plate).

Only animals which have been born and reared for their whole life on a Quality Meat Scotland Assured farm and slaughtered in a Quality Meat Scotland Assured abattoir, are eligible to be branded as Scotch Beef, Scotch Lamb or Specially Selected Pork.

Scotch Beef and Scotch Lamb were both awarded coveted PGI status by the European Union in 1996. PGI stands for Protected Geographical Indication and is a European programme to protect and promote high quality regional food products that are produced by traditional methods and have specific connections to their country of origin – in this case Scotland.

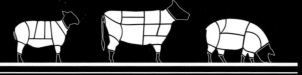

CUTS
OF MEAT

SCOTCH BEEF
Forequarter

The versatility of Scotch Beef is as infinite as your imagination. Due to the variety of cuts that Scotch Beef offers, the range of dishes you can prepare is huge. However, because of this very flexibility, all beef is not the same: different cuts require different cooking. The information opposite is a comprehensive snapshot of the most commonly used and prepared cuts.

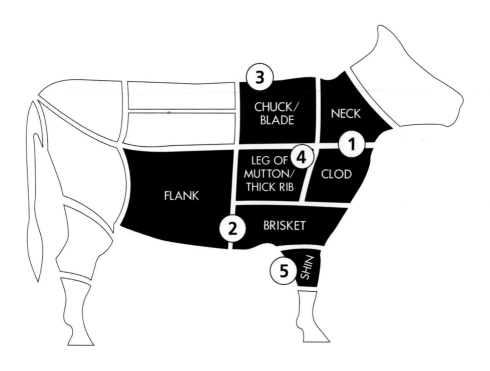

1. Neck and clod

Products: Diced.
Cooking methods: Stewing, casseroling, braising.

2. Flank / brisket

Products: Flank steak, roasting joints, short ribs.
Cooking methods: Ideal for moist, slow heat including stewing, braising and pot roasting. Also excellent for curing.

3. Chuck / blade

Products: Roasting joints and steaks when properly trimmed.
Cooking methods: Ideal for slow cooking such as casseroling, pot roasting, braising and slow roasting.

4. Leg of mutton / thick rib

Products: Diced, steaks (thinly sliced and served rare only to avoid poor eating experience).
Cooking methods: Frying, stewing, grilling, casseroling.

5. Shin

Products: Shin.
Cooking methods: Stewing, casseroling. (Ideal for osso buco).

The end of the animal's front legs, the shin, is generally inexpensive. It should be given plenty of time to cook slowly and can be obtained either on or off the bone. Foodies particularly enjoy the marrow in the bone - a very continental delicacy.

Scotch Beef
Hindquarter

The hindquarter provides the majority of tender steak cuts; fillet, sirloin and T-bone as well as the classic roasting joints, silverside, topside and rump.

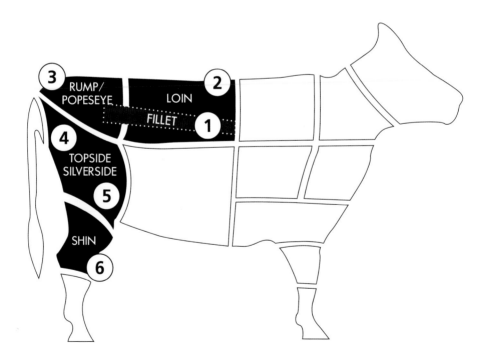

1. Fillet

Products: Cut into steaks or roasted whole.
Cooking methods: Grill, pan fry, roast. Fillet trimmings from the head, tail or chain are great for stir-frying or for a stroganoff. Add slivers to make tasty Thai beef soups.

2. Loin

Products: The loin is made up of various ribs which are well known as steaks e.g. sirloin, porterhouse, T-bone etc. Sirloin steak left on the bone with fillet attached is called T-bone.
Cooking methods: All generally are suitable for higher temperature methods of cooking such as pan frying, grilling or roasting.

3. Rump / popeseye

Products: Roasting joints or sliced into steaks. Pavé (French for paving stone and referring only to the shape) – is often used to describe a trimmed piece of rump that is very uniform and rectangular in shape.
Cooking methods: Rump is made up of three very different muscles – rump cap, rump heart (or eye) and rump tail. These muscles do vary in tenderness and can be cooked as roasts or sliced into high quality steaks. Rump heart being the tenderest.

4. Topside

Products: Roasting joints of various sizes.
Cooking methods: Topside is generally roasted. Suitable for either dry or wet roasting.

5. Silverside

Products: Roasting and curing in joints of various sizes.
Cooking methods: Silverside is another slow cooking or carvery joint. It is very lean and sometimes has a layer of pre-formed fat added to prevent the meat becoming too dry during cooking. Silverside is ideal for curing or salting. This can be either wet or dry cured using salt and a mixture of spices.

6. Shin

Products: Hough and shin.
Cooking methods: Stewing, casseroling or confit.
Shin, also known as leg of beef in England, is rich in collagen and connective tissue and has delicious marrow running through the hollow centre of the bone. It is essential to cook slowly at lower temperatures with plenty of moisture that will make a rich tasty sauce. Cut right through the bone, it is perfect for Osso buco.

Cook slowly on or off the bone until the meat falls away and press into a mould to make traditional Scottish potted hough.

Scotch Lamb
Tender and traditional

Scotch Lamb is a seasonal dish – at its very best during the late summer months, autumn and winter following the spring lambing period. Despite its image as a more expensive or fatty product, there are opportunities to source very economical cuts of Scotch Lamb which offer a range of delicious tastes. When combined with complimentary ingredients and cooked well the experience is sublime.

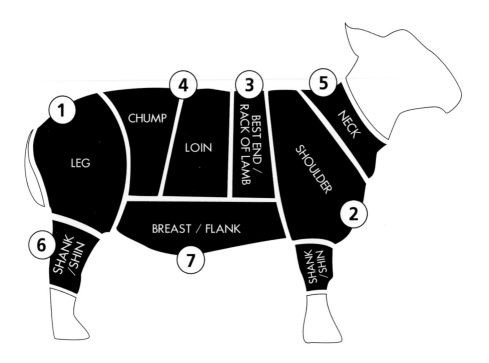

1 LEG · 4 CHUMP · LOIN · 3 BEST END / RACK OF LAMB · 5 NECK · SHOULDER · 2 · BREAST / FLANK · 6 SHANK / SHIN · 7 · SHANK / SHIN

1. Leg

Products: Joints, steaks, strips.
Cooking methods: Roast, pot roast, pan fry, stir-fry, grill, BBQ, stew.
Leg of lamb can be roasted bone-in or boned, rolled and tied with a stuffing of your choice.
Steaks can be grilled/pan fried whole or cut into strips for a stir-fry.

2. Shoulder

Products: Joints, steaks, diced (for stewing), mince.
Cooking methods: Roast, pot roast, pan fry, grill, BBQ, stew.
The shoulder joint should be cooked slower and longer than leg joints for a tender result.
Diced products could be marinated and skewered.

3. Best end / rack of lamb

Products: Joints, cutlets, noisettes.
Cooking methods: Roast, pan fry, grill, BBQ.
Ribs are often cut into little chops known as cutlets which can be grilled or pan fried.
Alternatively, the rack of lamb is the ultimate roasting joint for lamb lovers.

4. Chump and loin

Products: Joints, steaks, noisettes, chops, canon.
Cooking methods: Roast, pan fry, grill, BBQ.
Loins can be roasted but are more commonly available as quick cooking cuts as loin cuts
can be very lean.

5. Neck

Products: Joints, diced.
Cooking methods: Stew, casserole, slow braising.
Ideal for diced products, lamb neck provides fantastic meat for stews and curries.

6. Shank and shin

Products: Joints.
Cooking methods: Braising, casserole.
Lamb shanks are fairly lean and should be slow cooked whenever possible to allow the
strands of meat to come apart easily.

7. Breast / flank

Products: Joints, mince.
Cooking methods: Braising, casserole, slow roast.
Generally used most with a stuffing – slow roasted.

SPECIALLY SELECTED PORK
A modern product

As one of the world's favourite meats, pork has a special place in the heart of the keen chef. It's extremely versatile and fantastic value for money. In recent years, it's undoubtedly become more fashionable – perhaps helped by the fairly recent introduction of celebrity chef culture. When dealing with pork in the kitchen, you must always respect the cooking temperature and time to avoid the meat drying out. It's packed full of flavour with a generous fat cover which excels during slower cooking methods – with some cuts still working very well at higher temperatures for frying and grilling.

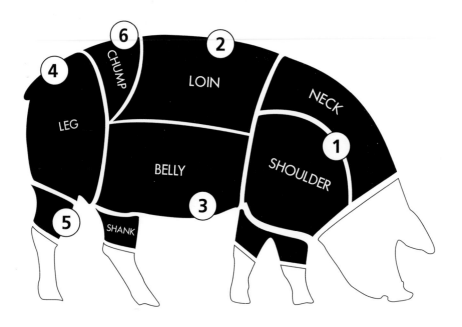

1. Neck and shoulder

Products: Joints, shoulder steaks, mince, sausages, diced (for casseroles).
Cooking methods: Roast, pot roast, pan fry, grill, BBQ, stew, soup, broth.
Slow cooked wherever possible to allow intramuscular fat to melt – keeping the meat moist.
Pork shoulder cuts can be roasted, used for steaks, diced or minced.

2. Loin

Products: Joints, loin steaks, back bacon.
Cooking methods: Roast, pan fry, grill, BBQ.
The loin delivers a number of roasting cuts with joints available both on and off the bone.
Alternatively, the loin is used for deliciously lean chops and steaks. The fillet (or tenderloin)
of pork is the delicate, lean piece of meat which runs through the loin.

3. Belly / flank

Products: Joints, steaks, mince, sausages, bacon, spare-ribs.
Cooking methods: Roast, pot roast, pan fry, grill, BBQ.
Ribs can be marinated in a delicious sauce, belly can be rolled, tied and oven roasted or
alternatively, sliced or cut into cubes. Cuts from the belly are fatty and as such offer great
taste and beautifully tender meat.

4. Leg

Products: Joints, leg steaks, escallopes, diced (for kebabs).
Cooking methods: Roast, pot roast, pan fry, grill, BBQ.
The leg is a lean piece of meat so be careful not to dry it out when cooking.

5. Knuckle / shank end

Products: Joints, mince.
Cooking methods: Roast, pot roast.
Pork shank is the lower part of the leg. It is usually prepared by pot roasting or oven
roasting slowly to retain the meat's tenderness. Shank is generally a cost efficient cut and
can add something very different to your menu.

6. Chump

Products: Joints and chops.
Cooking methods: Roast, pot roast, pan fry, grill, BBQ.
Chump chops are more generous than those from the loin. They're boneless, wider and
leaner, running up to the top of the leg. In joint format it can be roasted on or off the bone
and cooks to be slightly moister than the leg.

Why does meat colour vary?

Depending on certain atmospheric conditions, red meat can change colour quite significantly and appear anywhere between bright red and dark brown. This is due to concentrations in the air of various gases and how the meat pigment myoglobin reacts to these gases.

When meat is first cut from the carcass, it's a purplish-red colour because it hasn't been exposed to oxygen. It's the meat's reaction with the oxygen that turns it bright red. Red's good for beef and lamb, but slightly browner meat will often have a better taste and flavour.

The brown colour comes from being further exposed to oxygen and it's one of the signs of a well-aged piece of beef or lamb. Far from meaning the meat is going off, this colour is a natural part of the meat maturing – something that releases wonderful flavours.

If you purchase your meat in a vacuum-pack or skin pack the meat often appears to be a darker red, make sure you open the pack a good 20 minutes before cooking to allow the meat to come back to its full colour.

Marbling

Fat is critical to the flavour of meat and helps differentiate one meat from another. In fact, research has shown that if all traces of fat are stripped from a piece of lamb and a piece of beef, it is almost impossible to set them apart. Aside from the external layer of fat just beneath the surface of the skin, there is another presence of fat in the animals – this is called "marbling". This develops over time so is more predominant in beef or mutton than lamb or pork. In short, marbling is small streaks of intramuscular fat that are found in the muscle. It has a beneficial effect on juiciness and flavour by 'melting' through its surroundings during the cooking process.

Storing meat

It's especially important to store meat safely in the fridge to stop bacteria from spreading and avoid food poisoning.

* Store raw meat in clean, sealed containers on the bottom shelf of the fridge, so they can't touch or drip onto other food.
* Follow any storage instructions on the label and don't eat meat after its use-by date.
* Keep cooked meat separate from raw meat.

For more information contact the Food Standards Agency or visit their website.

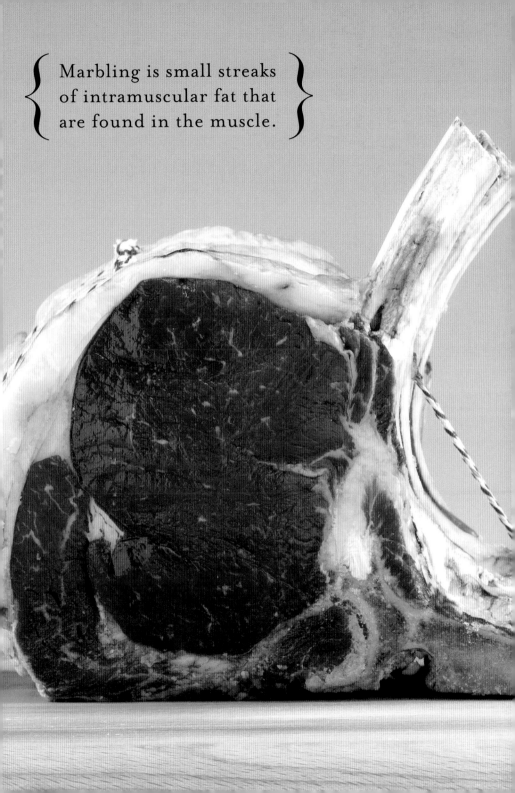

{ Marbling is small streaks of intramuscular fat that are found in the muscle. }

OFFAL

Recent interest in traditional and flavoursome food has increased consumer demand for products such as liver, heart, trotters and even tripe. An important part of our culinary heritage, offal provides an excellent source of iron and key vitamins to help with a healthy balanced diet. The wide range of offal products carry exactly the same quality and provenance assurances as the more mainstream cuts of Scotch Beef, Scotch Lamb and Specially Selected Pork. Specialist butchers have a range of excellent products to tempt you.

VEAL

Interest in veal is increasing and we're accustomed to seeing veal dishes in restaurants and in the media. Veal is an important part of Scotland's gastronomic heritage but it's only recently that we've rediscovered the possibilities. With a discreet flavour, veal is generally more tender than meat from older animals. Like beef, veal can be eaten as a simple steak or roast but its texture and taste allows a greater flexibility in the kitchen.

MUTTON

Much has been done in recent years to restore mutton's image as a very flavoursome product, full of character and open to gastronomic discovery. In general, mutton is perfect for slow cooking and roasting recipes, so why not discover or rediscover the flavour of mutton yourself?

WILD BOAR

Farmed wild boar, the ancestor to the domestic pig, has a long and colourful history. The meat is lean and exceptionally flavoursome ranging from mild and delicate to rich and gamey. The most tender cuts are from the loin but all cuts produce delicious results by utilising a range of cooking methods and accompaniments. Ideal for the expert and novice alike!

COOKING
MEAT

ROASTING

Traditional dry roasting is simply a great way to cook larger, tender cuts of meat.

Quantity

The current recommended maximum daily intake of red meat is around 80g cooked weight per person. Even at lower temperature cooking around 20% shrinkage will occur so allow approximately 120g (5ozs) raw meat per person if the joint is boneless and approximately 225g (8ozs) if the meat is on the bone. When calculating how much to buy, always add a little extra – a larger piece of meat will cook better and cold roast can make an easy meal with no cooking later in the week.

Basic recipe

The following simple recipe uses a lower roasting temperature to minimise the loss of moisture and shrinkage caused by cooking at higher temperatures.

* Allow the meat to come to room temperature and ensure that it is completely dry before cooking.

* Preheat the oven to the 180°C / 360°F / gas mark 4-5 (or turn down to 180°C if the meat has been browned in a very hot oven, see below).

* Brown the meat, either in a hot pan with a little vegetable oil or in a very hot oven 220°C / 425°F / gas mark 8 for 15 minutes.

* Once the meat has been browned, place it uncovered on a wire rack in a shallow roasting tin, ensuring that any fat is on the top.

* Continue to cook at 180°C / 360°F / gas mark 4-5 until it has reached the required internal temperature or level of "doneness" (see opposite).

Timing

The formula for roasting meat is based on minutes spent in the oven per kilo of meat.

Weigh the piece of meat before cooking and calculate the cooking time. If you are roasting a stuffed joint – weigh after stuffing. Use a skewer to test the juices' colour to indicate what stage the meat is at.

After the roast comes out of the oven, cover it with foil, (shiny side in) and allow it to rest for 10–15 minutes. This allows the meat to relax so the juices become evenly distributed throughout, making it succulent and easier to carve.

For detailed cooking times for beef, lamb and pork see pages 32 – 33 or download our free "Perfect Steaks and Roasts" app for iPhone, iPod Touch and Android.

RARE

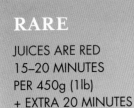

JUICES ARE RED
15–20 MINUTES
PER 450g (1lb)
+ EXTRA 20 MINUTES

MEDIUM

JUICES ARE PINK
22–25 MINUTES
PER 450g (1lb)
+ EXTRA 20 MINUTES

WELL DONE

JUICES ARE CLEAR
26–30 MINUTES
PER 450g (1lb)
+ EXTRA 20 MINUTES

* The above timings are for bone out. Images are all beef.

{ Resting allows the meat to relax so the juices become evenly distributed throughout, making it succulent and easier to carve. }

Pot roasting

Less tender cuts can also be roasted but require additional moisture and longer, slower cooking – usually covered for all or part of the cooking time.

Basic recipe

* Brown the piece of meat as before and place in a deep casserole/braising dish with vegetables, herbs and seasoning to add extra flavour.

* Root vegetables such as onion, carrot, turnip, celeriac, leek, celery and potato are ideal accompaniments and should be roughly cut into large chunks that will not break up during cooking. Mushrooms, peppers and tomatoes are also great but should be added when there is still 40 minutes of cooking time remaining.

* Allow approximately 450g (1lb) vegetables and 150ml (¼ pint) liquid, which can be water, stock, wine, cider, beer or a mixture for a 1.25kg (2½lb) joint.

* Cover tightly and cook slowly in a preheated oven at 180°C / 360°F / gas mark 4-5. Allow 30–40 minutes per 450g (1lb) plus an extra 20 minutes.

CASSEROLES

Casseroles are a great dish that can be served all year round. They are economical and a great way to cook meat and vegetables together. They are quick to prepare, freeze well and require little attention during cooking. Once you learn the basics, the variations are endless.

Basic recipe

* If your meat is not already cubed, remove any fat and cut into bite sized cubes.
* Place the cubes in a plastic bag and add plain seasoned flour (1tbsp per kilo of meat). Toss until the cubes of meat are completely coated. The flour will thicken the sauce during cooking.
* Heat a dessert spoon of vegetable oil in a large flameproof casserole dish or frying pan until very hot.
* Brown the cubes by adding a few pieces at a time to the hot dish. Do not add too many at one time. Remove the browned meat from the dish and set aside before browning the next batch. See pages 96 – 99 for a step by step guide to browning cubed steak.
* Sauté any fine cut vegetables such as onions, shallots and leeks then remove from the dish.
* Add 200ml of liquid. This could be meat or vegetable stock, red wine, beer, cider or even water. Use this to dissolve the cooking juices and loosen the meaty residues from the bottom and sides of the dish. This is called deglazing and is the basis for many sauces, once complete set aside in a jug.
* Place the browned meat and the sautéd vegetables back into the casserole dish; add some chunky, chopped seasonal root vegetables; season; pour over the deglazing liquid and additional stock so half the meat is covered and bring to a simmer.
* Put the lid on the casserole dish and place in a preheated oven around 140°C; 275°F; gas mark 1 and cook for between 2 and 3 hours or until the meat is tender.

Almonds and apricots are
a perfect accompaniment
for Scotch Lamb.

Variations

Casseroles are very versatile. Once you have mastered the basics the variations are endless.

* Be seasonal – vary the vegetables. Squash, peppers and mushroom all cook quickly, so add half way through cooking.

* Some other accompaniments that go well with meat;
  Scotch Beef – beetroot, blackberries and orange.
  Scotch Lamb – almonds, apricots and cherries.
  Specially Selected Pork – apple, apricots and plums.
  Add fruits to the casserole 30 minutes before serving.

* Vary your style of cuisine – traditional British, Indian and Asian curries, Mexican.

* Try adding port, honey or maple syrup for additional sweetness.

* For a bit more acidity - add a little lemon juice or cider vinegar (this can help if your casserole is a bit too salty).

* Tomatoes and tomato puree add both acidity and some sweetness, which gives fullness to the taste. Try paprika and a little cayenne for Hungarian dishes or olives and basil for Italian flavours.

* For more sweet and sour - add balsamic vinegar that has been reduced by two thirds, a tiny bit of honey and try some pineapple chunks too.

* Add herbs for colour and flavour. Parsley, thyme and coriander are great.

* 1 tablespoon of fresh chopped herbs = 1 teaspoon of dried herbs.

* Spice things up with a little chopped fresh chilli or for subtle flavour, pierce a red chilli and cook it in the casserole then remove it before serving.

* Cool things down with a generous spoonful of soured cream or half fat crème fraîche just before serving. A crumbling of feta cheese goes well with lamb and blue cheese is good with beef and pork.

GRILLING

A steak is a great treat, loved by all meat fans. There are many different cuts of steak to choose from including: fillet, sirloin, ribeye, rump, popeseye, T-bone, sirloin extra thin / sandwich steak, lamb steak or cutlet and pork chop or loin.

Basic recipe

Allow the steaks to come to room temperature before cooking. Trim any excess fat before cooking – but remember that fat gives flavour – so leave some on and remove before serving. Wash or wipe carefully, if required, and be sure to dry thoroughly with a paper towel. Any water that is present will reduce the cooking temperature and prevent browning. Control the salt – do not season before cooking – season to taste afterwards.

* Always preheat the grill or pan before starting to cook your steak.

* Grilling – position the grill pan approximately 5cm (2") away from the heat source and cook the steaks under a high heat. Turn only once.

* Pan frying – add a small amount of oil (5ml / 1tsp) to the pan and preheat to high.

* Be careful – the oil must be really hot but not smoking. Remember that different oils smoke (or haze) at different temperatures – vegetable oil can be heated higher than olive oil and butter will burn at a very low temperature.

* Griddle pans made of cast iron with a ridged base will create the look of barbeque char-grilled stripes and do not need to be oiled beforehand. Preheat to high and cook as if pan-frying.

* Do not over handle the steak. Whichever method you choose - turn only once, halfway through the calculated cooking time.

For detailed cooking times for beef, lamb and pork see pages 32 – 33 or download our free "Perfect Steaks and Roasts" app for iPhone, iPod Touch and Android.

Scotch Beef steaks

RARE

SEARED OUTSIDE
2½ MINS EACH SIDE
75% RED CENTRE
INTERNAL TEMP: 30–51°C

MEDIUM RARE

SEARED OUTSIDE
3–4 MINS EACH SIDE
50% RED CENTRE
INTERNAL TEMP: 57–63°C

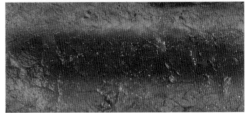

MEDIUM

SEARED OUTSIDE
4 MINS EACH SIDE
25% PINK CENTRE
INTERNAL TEMP: 63–68°C

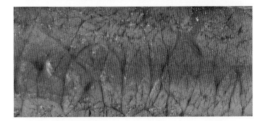

MEDIUM WELL

5 MINS EACH SIDE
SLIGHT HINT OF PINK
INTERNAL TEMP: 72–77°C

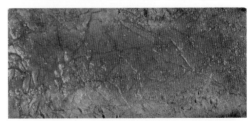

WELL DONE

6 MINS EACH SIDE
100% BROWN THROUGHOUT
INTERNAL TEMP: 77°C +

* The above examples are all beef and based on a 1″ sirloin steak, pan fried.

{ Allow the steaks to come to room temperature before cooking. }

COOKING TIMES

BEEF			
CUT	**COOKING**	**TEMPERATURE**	**TIMING**
Sirloin, Forerib, Topside, Silverside	Roast	180°C 350°F Gas mark 4-5	Rare - 20 mins per 450g plus 20 mins Medium - 25 mins per 450g plus 20 mins Well done - 30 mins per 450g plus 20 mins
Brisket	Pot roast or slow roast	180°C 350°F Gas mark 4-5	30–40 mins per 450g plus 30–40 mins
Stewing shoulder, Steak hough	Stew/ casserole	170°C 325°F Gas mark 3	2–3 hours
Prime casserole, Thick flank, Round steak	Casserole	170°C 325°F Gas mark 3	1–1½ hours
STEAKS			
Popeseye, Sirloin	Grill/fry	N/A	Rare - 2½ mins each side Medium - 4 mins each side Well done - 6 mins each side
Sirloin extra thin	Grill/fry	N/A	1 min each side
Fillet	Grill/fry	N/A	Rare - 3–4 mins each side Medium - 4–5 mins each side Well done - 6–7 mins each side

LAMB			
CUT	**COOKING**	**TEMPERATURE**	**TIMING**
Leg – whole or half boneless Shoulder – whole or boned and rolled, Half boneless loin, Best end neck	Roast	180°C 350°F Gas mark 4-5	Medium - 30 mins per 450g plus 30 mins Well done - 35 mins per 450g plus 30 mins
Loin chops	Grill/fry	N/A	4–6 mins each side
Chump chops	Grill/fry	N/A	4–6 mins each side
Leg steaks, Gigot chops	Grill/fry	N/A	4–6 mins each side
Cutlets	Grill/fry	N/A	4–6 mins each side
Shoulder lamb cubed	Grill Fry	N/A	3–5 mins each side 2–4 mins each side
Cube for kebabs	Grill	N/A	10–15 mins, turning occasionally

PORK

CUT	COOKING	TEMPERATURE	TIMING
Loin - bone in, Loin - boneless, Loin - chump end, Leg - whole/half, Leg - bone in roast, Leg - boneless, Streaky - joint (belly), Streaky - joint with stuffing (belly), Shoulder - joint, Boneless shoulder - shoulder joint with stuffing	Roast	180°C 350°F Gas mark 4-5	Medium - 30 mins per 450g plus 30 mins Well done - 35 mins per 450g plus 35 mins
Loin chops - bone in or boneless	Grill/fry		8–10 mins each side
Chump chops, gigot chops	Grill/fry		8–10 mins each side
Spare rib chops	Grill/fry		8–10 mins each side
Fillet slices (tenderloin) 1½ to 3cm thick 1 to 1½ cm thick	Grill/fry		3–5 mins each side 2–4 mins each side
Streaky rashers	Grill		4–5 mins each side
Belly slices	Roast	200°C 400°F Gas mark 6	25 mins
	Barbecue		20 mins, turning occasionally
	Grill		10–15 mins, turning occasionally

Download our free "Perfect Steaks and Roasts" app for iPhone, iPod Touch and Android.

Note: Cooking times may vary depending on thickness of cut. The Food Standards Agency suggest we limit the fat used in cooking. It is recommended to dry fry wherever possible.

COOKING MEAT

Accompaniments — stock, gravy and herbs

Basic stock recipe — Serves 4

Meat bones make the best flavoured stock and although time consuming it is absolutely worth it. You can use every last piece of meat and bones to help flavour the stock, there is no waste whatsoever. You can then freeze the stock in small portions to use as needed.

You will need

900g meat bones (beef, veal, lamb or pork)

2 sprigs of thyme

2 sprigs of parsley

1 large bay leaf

2 onions, roughly chopped

2 celery sticks, roughly chopped

2 carrots, roughly chopped

5 peppercorns

Place the bones in a large saucepan and add about 2 litres of water, enough to cover the bones. Bring to the boil, skimming off the scum as it rises to the surface.

Tie the thyme, parsley, bay leaf into a bouquet garni and add to the pan with the onions, celery, carrots and peppercorns. Cover and simmer gently for 5 – 6 hours.

Strain the stock through a sieve into a bowl, discarding the bones and vegetables. Leave to cool, then chill until the fat has risen to the surface of the stock and solidified. Lift the fat off the surface and discard before using the stock.

Further stock ideas

* To make a richer, brown stock, roast the bones in a hot oven (230°C, 450°F, gas mark 8) for 40 minutes.

* For a boneless stock, brown a 125g piece of stewing beef, lean boneless lamb or pork in 1tbsp sunflower oil in a large saucepan. Remove the meat, and add a roughly chopped onion, carrot and celery stick to the pan. Brown the vegetables, then pour in 2 litres of water and bring to the boil. Add the meat and heat until simmering again, skim off any fat, add 2 bay leaves, a sprig of parsley and thyme, 10 black peppercorns and ½tsp salt. Reduce the heat, cover and simmer for 2 hours. Strain, cool and remove any fat. This will make about 1.2 litres of stock.

* After chilling the stock you can boil it until reduced and concentrated in flavour, then cool and freeze it. Ice-cube trays are a great way to store stock then you can simply add them frozen to your hot soup, casserole or stew and they will melt in with all their lovely flavours. Taste constantly to check the correct strength of flavour has been achieved, it's easy to add an extra frozen cube of stock as you go.

Gravy

For a simple thick gravy, when the meat has been removed from its roasting tray, discard any excess fat then add 1–2tbsp of gravy granules to the meat juices and cook, stirring all the time until thickened. Adjust the consistency with water or stock and serve. Remember to scrape the sediment from the sides and base of the pan to release the meaty flavour.

Alternatively, sprinkle 1tbsp of plain flour into the pan, mix well with the juices and cook over a medium heat. Stir well with a spoon or small whisk and add the additional liquid a little at a time until thickened. Adjust the seasoning and simmer to cook the flour for 8 – 10 minutes.

Other accompaniments

Beef – Creamy blue cheese sauce, combine natural yoghurt with a good blue vein cheese and chopped spring onions. For a hot chilli accompaniment, mix natural yoghurt, tomatoes and chillis.

Lamb – Slivers of garlic, sprigs of rosemary and/or anchovies can be pushed into slits cut in the meat. Try grinding grated lemon rind, root ginger and garlic, or mint and rosemary, into a paste to fill the slits. Flavoured butters also work well with lamb steaks and chops. Make by simply softening butter and folding through the grated rind of a lemon or lime, some thyme and rosemary. Or try some chilli paste and a few leaves of freshly torn basil.

Pork – There are many spices and seasonings which work well with pork. Consider accompaniments such as peach, apricot or pineapple. Sage, rosemary and thyme complement the wide range of pork cuts available.

Herbs

It is not always possible to grow everything you need all year round so having some essential dried herbs and spices in the cupboard will extend the range of recipes you can create.

Dried herbs are more concentrated than fresh herbs, so you need to use less. The recommended conversion is to substitute teaspoons for tablespoons - 2 teaspoons of dried oregano is the equivalent of 2 tablespoons of fresh.

Sometimes dried herbs cannot be substituted, for example you wouldn't want to use dried herbs to make pesto. Generally, if fresh herbs are a main component of the dish the less successful dried herbs will be.

Remember, ground ginger cannot be used as a substitute for root ginger, their flavours are completely different.

Sauces, stews and casseroles can be very successfully flavoured with dried herbs.

Beef – allspice, basil, bay, garlic, ginger, marjoram, oregano & thyme.

Lamb – mint, dill, garlic, rosemary.

Pork – caraway seeds, coriander, cumin, dill, garlic, rosemary, sage, fennel & thyme.

For ideas on pairing ingredients for beef, lamb and pork, see the table on page 38.

LEFTOVERS

Buying only what you need while it's fresh and in season is a great way to experience the very best quality produce and maximise your shopping budget. There is much more to beef, lamb and pork than a one-off roast dinner.

To make the most of every last piece leftovers can be used for dinners, lunches or light meals and are very handy to have up your sleeve. Excellent in curries, salads, sandwiches, pasta dishes, soups and stocks. The options really are endless and allows you to use any leftover meat you may have from your roast to give you two or even three different meal occasions.

Pairing ingredients

Some interesting flavour combinations to try with beef, lamb and pork.

	BEEF	LAMB	PORK
Almond		•	
Anchovy	•	•	
Anise	•	•	•
Apple			•
Apricot		•	•
Artichoke (Globe)		•	•
Artichoke (Jerusalem)	•		•
Aubergine		•	
Bacon	•		•
Beans		•	•
Beetroot	•		•
Bell pepper	•		
Blackberry	•		
Black pudding	•	•	•
Blue cheese	•		•
Caper	•	•	
Cardamom		•	•
Cherry		•	
Chestnut		•	•
Chilli	•		•
Cinnamon	•	•	•
Clove	•		•
Cocoa	•		
Coconut	•		•
Coffee	•		•
Coriander leaf		•	•
Cucumber	•	•	•
Egg	•		•
French beans	•		•
Foie gras	•		•
Garlic	•	•	•

	BEEF	LAMB	PORK
Ginger	•		•
Goat's cheese		•	
Grape	•		•
Grapefruit			•
Haggis	•	•	•
Hard cheese	•		
Horseradish	•		
Juniper	•		•
Lemon	•	•	
Lime	•		
Liver	•		
Mustard	•		
Nutmeg		•	
Oily fish	•		•
Olive	•		
Orange	•		
Oyster	•	•	•
Peanut	•	•	•
Pear	•		•
Pepper	•	•	•
Pineapple			•
Prune			•
Rhubarb		•	•
Shellfish	•	•	•
Swede	•	•	•
Tea	•	•	•
Tomato	•	•	•
Truffle	•		•
Walnut	•		
Watercress	•		•
Watermelon			•

BEEF
RECIPES

SERVES **3** PREPARATION **15** mins COOKING **15** mins

BEEF STIR-FRY

You will need

300g Scotch Beef sirloin steak, trimmed of fat and sliced into thin strips

2 cloves garlic, finely chopped

3tbsp groundnut oil

3 spring onions, diagonally sliced

1 red pepper, cut into thin strips

80g tenderstem broccoli

1 large carrot, cut into matchsticks

80g sugarsnap peas, sliced lengthwise

1tbsp ginger, finely chopped

1tsp red chilli, finely chopped

100g bean sprouts, rinsed and drained

100g chestnut or oyster mushrooms, sliced

3tbsp light soy sauce and 3 tbsp water

5tbsp oyster sauce

Plain boiled brown basmati rice to serve

Sprinkle the chopped garlic over the steak slices and set aside.

Heat half the oil in a wok or non-stick pan and fry the onions, carrot, and broccoli for 2 minutes while stirring. Add the red pepper and sugar snap peas and stir-fry for a minute before adding the chopped ginger and chilli, followed by the bean sprouts and mushrooms. Toss all together and then add the soy sauce and water. Shake the pan then put on a lid and steam the vegetables for 2 or 3 minutes until tender, but still with a little bite.

Heat another pan, add the remaining oil and when "shimmery hot" toss in the garlic beef and stir-fry for a minute till brown, then add the oyster sauce and stir to coat the beef. Remove from the heat.

Serve a nice big pile of vegetables on each plate, topped with the succulent glazed beef slices and some rice if you like.

SERVES
10

 PREPARATION
20 mins

 COOKING
2½ hrs

ROAST RIB OF BEEF

You will need

3kg rib of Scotch Beef on the bone

2tbsp olive oil

1kg shallots, peeled and halved lengthwise

3 heads garlic, cut in half widthwise

Juice of 2 oranges

3tbsp wholegrain mustard

3tbsp light muscovado sugar

Leaves from 6 sprigs of thyme

2tsp coarse flakes of sea salt

Freshly ground black pepper

Finely grated zest of ½ orange

Preheat the oven to 220°C.

Weigh the joint and calculate the cooking time –
15 minutes per 500g plus 30 minutes for rare beef;
20 minutes per 500g plus 30 minutes for medium;
25 minutes per 500g plus 30 for well done.

In a large roasting tin, toss the shallots and garlic with the oil and roast for 15 minutes.

Pour the orange juice over the shallots.

Meanwhile, with a very sharp knife score a criss-cross pattern deeply into the fat of the beef, but not through to the flesh. Mix together the mustard, sugar, thyme, salt, pepper and orange zest and rub this mixture all over the beef but particularly between the cuts. Set the beef on top of the shallots and return to the oven. After 15 minutes, reduce the oven temperature to 180°C.

Check every now and again that the beef is not browning too quickly and that the shallots and garlic are slightly moist, add 100ml of water if necessary, and cover the beef loosely with a double sheet of greaseproof paper. Once cooked allow the meat to rest covered with foil for 15 minutes, in a warm place, before carving thinly.

Serve with the soft shallots and vegetables of your choice.

FILLET OF BEEF

with wild mushrooms and Prosciutto

You will need

500g piece of Scotch Beef fillet (middle cut)

8 slices Parma ham (Prosciutto) or 1 x 90g pack sliced Prosciutto

For the mushroom paste

15g dried mixed wild mushrooms

250g button chestnut mushrooms, finely chopped

25g unsalted butter

2 shallots, peeled and finely chopped

1 clove garlic, crushed

½tsp thyme leaves

3tbsp double cream

10 pitted black olives, sliced

2tbsp parsley, chopped

Soak the dried mushrooms in warm water for 20 minutes then drain and squeeze out any remaining moisture, and finely chop them.

Soften the shallot and garlic in the butter and oil in a broad based pan over a gentle heat until transparent, but not brown (5 minutes), then add all the chopped mushrooms, increase the heat slightly and fry for about 10 minutes until all the moisture has evaporated. Add the thyme leaves and just a hint of salt and pepper. Add the cream, stir, and remove from the heat. Cool a little then chop in a food processor till a fine paste but still with some texture.

Heat the oven to 190°C. Lightly season the fillet then sear it on all sides in a very hot non-stick pan, with no oil, (5 – 6 minutes). Cool.

Oil a sheet of baking parchment then overlay the ham slices, 2 across (widthways) and 4 down to make a sheet that will wrap all the way round the meat. Spread the mushroom paste evenly over this, leaving a margin on the short ends to tuck under the joint. Sprinkle the parsley and olives over this.

Place the meat at one side of the Prosciutto 'blanket' and with the help of the paper roll up the beef and transfer to a roasting tin, carefully removing the paper. Put in the oven for 30 – 40 minutes, for a medium rare result. Allow the meat to rest for 10 minutes before cutting into thick slices.

BEEF SATAY

with peanut dipping sauce

You will need

600g Scotch Beef ribeye or sirloin steak, trimmed of all fat and sinew

24 bamboo satay sticks, soaked in water

For the marinade

2tsp grated fresh ginger

1 clove garlic, crushed

1tbsp dark soy sauce

1tbsp clear honey

½tsp dried chilli flakes

2tsp sesame oil

Juice and finely shredded zest of half lime

For the Peanut Dipping Sauce

160ml canned coconut milk

4tbsp crunchy peanut butter (buy a good quality, preferably organic one)

1tsp red chilli, chopped

1tbsp soy sauce

Juice of half lime

1tbsp spring onion, finely chopped

1tbsp coriander leaves, chopped

Basmati rice or crispy rice noodles to serve

Mix together all the marinade ingredients in a bowl big enough to hold the steak (keep a little of the marinade aside for brushing during cooking). Slice the steak into long strips, 1cm wide and tip into the marinade, making sure all is well coated. Set aside while you prepare the dipping sauce.

Put all the sauce ingredients, except the lime juice, into a small saucepan but don't heat yet. Chop up the onion and coriander and set aside.

Set the grill to its highest setting. Thread the beef in wiggly shapes onto the soaked skewers. If you are serving rice, start cooking it now, then when the grill is ready, grill the skewers in a single layer, turning two or three times until they look browned and sticky, brush with remaining marinade when turning.

Gently heat the pan with the sauce ingredients, stirring constantly until the ingredients are melted and the sauce thickened and hot, do not boil. Remove from the heat and stir in the lime juice. Taste, and if you'd like it saltier, add a little more soy sauce, a couple of drops at a time. Transfer to a serving bowl.

Serve the satay with a sprinkling of chopped coriander and spring onion and the dipping sauce, and rice or crispy noodles (or a tomato and onion salad would counteract the richness).

SERVES
4

PREPARATION
20 mins

COOKING
15 mins

EASY ASIAN BEEF NOODLE SOUP

You will need

250g fillet of Scotch Beef (cut from the narrow end), thinly sliced

600ml liquid beef stock

2tbsp light soy sauce

2tbsp chilli sauce

2cm piece ginger, peeled and cut into matchsticks

2 carrots, peeled and cut into matchsticks

100g tight white button mushrooms, sliced

2 heads pak choi, thinly sliced

Fresh sweetcorn cut from 1 cob

2 bundles rice noodles (about 100g)

4 spring onions, shredded

2tsp toasted sesame oil

1tbsp toasted sesame oil to serve

Into a large broad based pan pour the stock, soy sauce, chilli sauce and ginger and bring to the boil.

Add the carrots and mushrooms and cook for 2 minutes; add the corn, noodles and pak choi and simmer for 3 minutes. Then add the beef slices and shredded onion and heat through to just set the beef. Stir in the sesame oil and serve the soup in bowls with some sesame seeds sprinkled over each.

SZECHUAN STYLE ORANGE BEEF

You will need

2 Scotch Beef fillet steaks (150g each)

2tbsp groundnut or sunflower oil

150g shiitake mushrooms, thinly sliced

1 orange, peel and pith removed and cut into segments

For the marinade

2tbsp light soy sauce

1tbsp fine cut orange marmalade

1tbsp clear honey

Juice of 1 orange

1tbsp Shaoxing rice wine

½tsp Szechuan pepper, crushed

Watercress and cucumber salad to serve

Make the marinade by mixing all the ingredients together. Put the steaks in the marinade and turn them to coat thoroughly and rub in the Szechuan pepper.

Heat a deep non-stick sauté pan or wok until the oil is just beginning to smoke (don't allow to burn). Shake excess marinade from the steaks and sear in the hot oil for 2 minutes before turning to sear the other side, cook 2 more minutes then add the remaining marinade mixture, turning the steaks until coated in the sticky sauce. Remove the meat to two warm plates and spoon over the sauce from the pan. Steam the mushrooms in the traces of sauce left in the pan with 3tbsp water added, until soft and aromatic. Spoon around the steaks.

Dress the finished dish with watercress, slivers of cucumber and the orange segments. No salad dressing will be needed.

SERVES **4** PREPARATION **25** mins COOKING **30** mins

RATHER SPECIAL BEEF BURGER

You will need

450g Scotch Beef ribeye, coarsely ground

Small red onion, finely chopped

2tbsp chopped herbs such as parsley, chives, marjoram

4 Ciabatta buns, the olive ones are great

For caramelised onions

3 medium red onions, peeled, thinly sliced

25g unsalted butter

2tbsp olive oil

Pinch of salt

Pinch of sugar

For blue cheese dressing

100g semisoft blue cheese such as Roquefort

100ml soured cream

To serve

Mixed baby salad leaves

1 large tomato, cut into 8 slices

Start with the caramelised onions. Fry the onions in the oil and butter over a gentle heat until transparent and soft (6 minutes) then sprinkle on the salt and sugar and continue cooking, stirring from time to time until golden and sticky and beginning to crisp at the edges. Set aside.

Mix together all the burger ingredients and season. Mixing them with your hands makes it easier. Shape into 4 burgers about 10 – 12cm diameter.

Heat the grill to its hottest setting and cook the burgers for 3 – 4 minutes on each side for rare, 4 – 5 minutes for medium and 5 – 6 minutes for well done.

Pop the split ciabatta buns under the grill to warm a little.

Load up the buns with a handful of salad leaves, a couple of tomato slices, a burger, a tangle of onions and a dollop of blue cheese dressing for those who'd like it.

BEEF CARPACCIO TARTLETS

You will need

450g piece of Scotch Beef fillet, trimmed of any fat and sinew

2tsp mixed peppercorns, pounded in a mortar and pestle

1tbsp rosemary, finely chopped

2 pinches salt

1 small raw beetroot, peeled

1 medium carrot, peeled

100g celeriac, peeled

2tbsp extra virgin olive oil

2tbsp balsamic vinegar

Salt

Hot horseradish sauce

8 small basil leaves

For the tartlets

200g plain flour

100g cold, unsalted butter, cut into cubes

25g finely grated parmesan

2tbsp cold water

10cm mini tart tins, buttered

To make the pastry, put the flour, butter and cheese into a food processor and pulse until like fine breadcrumbs, add the water and pulse again to combine. Remove from the processor and pinch together with your fingers, chill while you sear the meat.

Mix the pepper, rosemary and salt together on a flat surface and roll the beef firmly in it to evenly coat the surface. Heat a griddle to very hot and brown the meat on all sides, 5 – 6 minutes. (The best way to do this is to use long handled tongs to steady the meat when browning). Remove to a board to cool.

Heat the oven to 200°C and place a baking sheet on the middle shelf.

Thinly roll out the pastry and use to line the mini tins. Prick the pastry bases with a fork and press some buttered foil into the cases to prevent the pastry sliding whilst cooking. Bake for 10 minutes, carefully remove foil and finish cooking a further 10 minutes until the pastry is crisp and golden brown. Cool a little in the tins then remove to a cooling rack.

If you have a mandolin grater, cut the vegetables into very fine julienne strips, do the beetroot last! If not, cut each into very thin slices and then cut those into very thin matchsticks, leaving them in three separate piles. In a small bowl mix together the oil, vinegar and salt and set aside.

Slice the beef as thinly as humanly possible with a very sharp knife. It doesn't matter if the slices break up a bit, it will melt in the mouth. Carefully arrange a couple of slices into each of the pastry cases with a pile of the little vegetable sticks next to them. Dress the vegetables with some oil and balsamic and the beef with a trail of the horseradish. Top each with a basil leaf.

LAMB
RECIPES

SERVES
4

 **PREPARATION**
15 mins

 **COOKING**
30 mins

MUSTARD & HERB CRUSTED LAMB

with pea puree

You will need

2 Scotch Lamb racks, French trimmed

50g dry white bread

1 clove garlic, crushed

2tbsp fresh parsley, chopped

2tbsp fresh mint, chopped

2tbsp olive oil

2tbsp pine nuts

Salt and freshly ground black pepper

2tbsp wholegrain mustard

Olive oil and a sprig of mint to garnish

For the Pea Puree

A knob of butter

1 small leek, trimmed and sliced

225g frozen peas

A sprig of mint

150ml chicken stock

3tbsp double cream

A little freshly grated nutmeg

Preheat the oven to 200°C.

Place the racks in a large roasting tin.

Place the bread and garlic in a food processor and blend until the bread forms fine crumbs. Add the herbs and oil and blend again until roughly chopped. Lastly, add the pine nuts and blend briefly until lightly chopped. The mixture should stick together lightly.

Spread the mustard over the lamb rack, then press the herb crust onto each one, pressing it down firmly so it sticks. Roast for 25 minutes in the centre of the oven. This gives medium cooked lamb - for more well done cook for a further 10 minutes.

Meanwhile, make the pea puree: melt the butter in a medium pan, add the leek and sauté for 3 – 4 minutes or until soft. Add the peas, mint and stock, bring to the boil, cover and simmer for 4 minutes. Use a stick blender to whizz the pea mixture to form a rough puree. Add the cream and nutmeg and season to taste.

Remove the lamb from the oven and leave to rest for 5 minutes.

Carve the lamb into cutlets. Divide the pea puree between four warm plates, top with the lamb cutlets. To garnish, drizzle a little olive oil on each plate and add a sprig of mint.

ROLLED LAMB SHOULDER

with basil and pine nuts

You will need

1 boned shoulder of Scotch Lamb weighing 1.3kg

4tbsp pine nuts

50g fresh basil

2 cloves garlic, peeled and chopped

75g pitted green olives

Salt and freshly ground black pepper

500g charlotte potatoes

2 red peppers, deseeded and cut into chunks

2 red onions, cut into wedges

Preheat the oven to 220°C.

Place the pine nuts, basil, garlic and olives on a large board, then use a large sharp knife to chop them all together until you have a rough paste. Season with salt and plenty of ground black pepper.

Unroll the boned shoulder and place skin side down on a board. Scatter the basil paste over the meat, rubbing it into all the crevices and cut surfaces. Roll up the shoulder of lamb and tie it together with string at regular intervals to make a neat parcel.

Place the lamb in the centre of a large roasting tin. Roast for 10 minutes. Reduce the temperature to 180°C and roast for 40 minutes.

Remove the roasting tin from the oven, add all the vegetables and toss together until coated in the pan juices. Roast for a further 40 minutes.

Transfer the meat to a board and leave to rest for 10 minutes, covered with foil. Keep the vegetables warm in a serving dish.

To serve, thickly slice the lamb and serve with the roasted vegetables.

LAMB CHUMP ROAST

with a ginger and rosemary glaze

You will need

1 Scotch Lamb chump, scored, boned and rolled (approx 500g, boned weight)

Ask your butcher to prepare this uncommon little gem for you.

For the glaze

1 tsp rosemary, finely chopped

2 pieces of stem ginger preserved in syrup, finely chopped

1 tbsp of the ginger syrup

Salt and pepper

Preheat the oven to 180°C.

Place the meat in a small roasting tin. Mix together all the glaze ingredients and keep half aside for later, brush the other half of it over the joint of lamb. Cover loosely with a double sheet of baking parchment so that the syrup doesn't burn. Put into the hot oven for 25 minutes.

Re-glaze the meat with the remaining mixture and return to the oven for 30 minutes, covered with the paper. Remove the paper for the last 10 minutes of the cooking time. Transfer the lamb to a warm serving plate and cover with foil to rest for 10 – 15 minutes before carving.

Cook's tip: Simmer some whole peeled small onions in lightly salted water until tender, then using this "onion stock", make a white sauce (in the usual way with butter and flour), season with lots of black pepper and return the onions to the pan to heat through, and serve this onion sauce and some wilted spinach and sliced lamb.

SERVES
10

PREPARATION
15 mins

COOKING
3 hrs 45 mins

SLOW COOKED LAMB
with lemony potatoes

You will need

2kg leg of Scotch Lamb

2 onions, peeled and chopped

1tsp salt

1tsp ground black pepper

Juice of 1 lemon

2 cloves garlic, crushed

4tbsp olive oil

3tbsp red currant jelly

For the potatoes

1.5kg potatoes, peeled and cut into large chunks

2 cloves garlic, crushed

2tbsp fresh oregano, chopped

Juice of 1 lemon

150ml extra virgin olive oil

Preheat the oven to 220°C.

Place the lamb in a non-corrosive ovenproof dish on a bed of chopped onions. Whisk together the salt, pepper, lemon juice, garlic, olive oil, redcurrant jelly and 150ml water and pour it over the lamb. Season the lamb with a little salt, cover the whole thing closely with foil and put in the oven for 30 minutes while you prepare the potatoes.

In another non-corrosive ovenproof dish large enough to hold all the potatoes in a single layer and the lamb (which you will add later), tip in the potatoes and sprinkle them with the garlic and oregano and pour over the lemon juice and oil. Barely cover the potatoes with cold water and season with salt and pepper.

Place the potato tray in the oven when the lamb's first 30 minutes has elapsed, and continue cooking for 15 minutes before reducing the oven temperature to 150°C, without opening the oven door. Cook for a further hour.

Turn over the potatoes in their liquid, lift the lamb to sit, other side up, on top of the potatoes. Spoon off and discard any visible oil from the surface of the meat juices then pour the remainder and the onions over the lamb and potatoes. Cover loosely with foil and return to the middle of the oven for a further hour (or more) or until the potatoes are soft and golden tinged brown and the lamb, very tender.

Serve cut into thick slices, spoon on some of the soft lemon potatoes and their delicious juices.

LAMB MOUSSAKA

You will need

500g lean Scotch Lamb mince

1 onion, chopped

1 clove garlic, crushed

3tbsp tomato puree

2tbsp mint jelly

2 aubergines

75g feta cheese

500g Greek yogurt

2 eggs

In a non-stick pan dry fry the mince for 4 – 5 minutes with the onion and garlic. Add the tomato puree and mint jelly. Season with salt and pepper and cook for 2 – 3 minutes.

Meanwhile thinly slice the aubergines and lightly brown on both sides in a hot frying pan (you might have to do this in two or three batches).

Place half the mince mixture into an ovenproof dish and top with some of the aubergine slices. Crumble over the feta cheese and cover with the rest of the mince and the remaining aubergine.

Mix together the Greek yogurt with the eggs and pour over the aubergines.

Bake in a preheated oven for 30 – 35 minutes until golden brown.

Serve with a baked Greek salad - roast tomatoes, slices of red onion and olives topped with crumbled feta cheese.

GRIDDLED LAMB STEAKS
with Greek salad

You will need

2 Scotch Lamb gigot (leg) steaks
Salt and pepper

For the salad
2 large tomatoes, cut into chunks
½ small cucumber, peeled, cut into chunks

1 small red onion, very thinly sliced
50g Kalamata olives
50g feta cheese, broken into small pieces
Leaves from 2 sprigs oregano, roughly torn
Black pepper and olive oil to dress

Mix together all the salad ingredients except the oil.

Heat a non-stick griddle pan to medium/hot. Lightly season both steaks and place them on the hot pan at a diagonal to the stripes for 2 – 3 minutes then turn 90 degrees to achieve a criss-cross pattern. Turn and cook the other sides in the same way, 2 – 3 minutes, then a further 2 – 3 minutes or until the lamb is cooked to your liking. (Remove the steaks to a warm oven for 5 – 10 minutes if you prefer the lamb to be well done.)

Dress the salad with a good extra virgin olive oil and serve with the gigot steaks and warm crusty bread.

SPICY LAMB CURRY

with aubergine and butternut squash

You will need

800g Scotch Lamb shoulder meat, cut into bite-sized pieces

4tbsp vegetable oil

2 onions, peeled and thickly sliced

2 cloves garlic, peeled and crushed

2.5cm piece ginger, peeled and grated

1tsp coriander seeds, crushed

1tsp cumin seeds, crushed

2tbsp medium-hot curry paste

1tbsp plain flour

750ml water or vegetable stock

1 large aubergine, cut into 2cm cubes

500g butternut squash, cut into 2cm cubes

4 tomatoes, quartered

2tbsp mango chutney

Small handful chopped coriander leaves

Preheat the oven to 160°C.

Gently fry the onion and garlic in one tablespoon of the oil for 3 or 4 minutes until softened, add the ginger and spices, fry for a minute more then transfer to an oven proof casserole dish.

Increase the heat under the frying pan, add one more tablespoon of the oil and fry the meat, in batches, until brown on all sides, about 6 minutes for each batch. Transfer to the casserole dish with the onions. Add the curry paste and flour to the last batch of browned meat and fry for one minute more before adding some of the water or stock and stirring well to get up all the flavoursome morsels that have stuck to the pan. Tip all this into the casserole dish.

Add the rest of the liquid to the curry, bring to the boil and season with salt, then cover with the lid and cook in the oven for about 40 minutes until the meat is almost tender.

Meanwhile, over a medium heat fry the aubergine cubes in a little extra oil for 5 minutes until lightly golden but not cooked through.

Add the aubergine, butternut squash, tomatoes and chutney to the curry and return to the oven for 25 minutes until the meat and squash are very tender. Check the seasoning.

Sprinkle with the coriander and serve with poppadums, rice and extra chutney.

LAMB EN CROÛTE

You will need

200g Scotch Lamb neck fillet, the thickest end

Salt and pepper

1 egg, lightly beaten

½ sheet ready-rolled puff pastry (from a 375g pack)

1 tbsp ready made tomato and olive tapenade

Trim any excess fat and sinew from the fillet. Season with salt and pepper and dry fry in a non-stick pan for a few seconds on all sides until seared and brown all over. Set aside to cool thoroughly.

Preheat the oven to 200°C. Line a baking tray with baking parchment.

Roll the pastry a little thinner and trim to fit the meat with plenty left to overlap and seal without stretching it. Cut a couple of leaf shapes from the off-cuts.

Spread the tapenade all over the cooled lamb and place it in the middle of the pastry, brush the pastry edges with beaten egg and fold over the meat enclosing it in a well sealed, neat rectangular parcel. Place on the baking tray and brush the pastry all over with beaten egg. Chill in the fridge for a few minutes for the pastry to firm up.

Lightly score the pastry in a cross hatched pattern without making any holes. Brush the pastry leaves with egg and stick on top of the parcel.

Place in the oven for 10 minutes then reduce the temperature to 180°C for a further 15 – 20 minutes until the pastry is well risen and a rich golden brown. Cover with a double sheet of baking parchment if you think the pastry is colouring too quickly. Remove from the oven and leave to rest for 15 minutes or so before cutting in half and serving with your favourite vegetables or a crisp leafy salad. The flavour will be better if the parcel is allowed to cool a little before serving.

PORK
RECIPES

SERVES **4** PREPARATION **15** mins  COOKING **20** mins

SKEWERED PORK FILLET

with sage and apple

You will need

450g Specially Selected Pork fillet, or lean shoulder, cut into 2cm slices

2 small Cox or Braeburn apples, cored and cut into wedges

2 small red onions, peeled, cut into quarters lengthwise, layers separated

12 sage leaves

For the marinade

3tbsp olive oil

2tbsp cider vinegar (or 6tbsp apple juice)

1 clove garlic peeled and crushed

2tsp dried oregano or mixed herbs

Salt and pepper

8 bamboo or metal skewers

Prepare the meat, apples and onions as above and place in a bowl.

Combine all the ingredients for the marinade (reserve a little for brushing during cooking), pour the rest over the prepared meat etc, and leave to marinate for 20 – 30 minutes, turning in the liquid now and again.

Preheat the grill or light the barbeque.

Thread the skewers with a chunk of meat, a slice of onion, a sage leaf and a piece of apple; and so on until you've used up all the ingredients. Reserve the marinade to brush over the kebabs as they cook.

Cook under a hot grill (or BBQ) for about 15 – 20 minutes, turning regularly and brushing with the marinade until done to your liking. Let the kebabs rest for 5 minutes or so before eating.

Serve with rice or in a warm baguette with mustard and watercress.

PORK CHOPS
with rosemary and ginger-wine sauce

You will need

4 x 200g Specially Selected Pork chops, trimmed of excess fat, or 4 boneless Specially Selected Pork loin steaks

Salt and pepper

12tbsp green ginger wine

200ml water or stock

Leaves from 2 rosemary sprigs, finely chopped

A little olive oil or butter

2tbsp grainy mustard

1tbsp finely chopped parsley

Leafy salad

Warm crusty bread

4tbsp cream or half fat crème fraîche (optional)

Sprinkle the chops with the rosemary, salt and pepper.

Heat a non-stick frying pan until nice and hot then add a teaspoon of oil or a knob of butter. Fry the chops for 6 – 7 minutes on each side until well browned. Remove the chops to a warm serving dish in a moderate oven while you make the sauce.

Reduce the heat then pour in the ginger wine, let it bubble for a few seconds then add the water or stock and simmer until the liquid is reduced by half.

Stir in the mustard, cream (if using) and parsley. After another minute remove from the heat.

Check that the chops are thoroughly cooked (those with the bone in will take a little longer than the loin steaks) and if not quite done you can return them to the pan with the sauce and simmer gently for a few minutes more.

Serve the chops with plenty of sauce spooned over and crusty bread to mop up the juices.

SERVES 2 PREPARATION 5 mins  COOKING 20 mins

PAN-FRIED PORK MEDALLIONS

with honeyed plums

You will need

200g Specially Selected Pork fillet, trimmed of any sinews

2tbsp liquid honey

Juice and finely grated rind of ½ orange

Juice of half a lime

A little olive oil

Salt and black pepper

3 ripe but firm plums, cut in half, stones removed

1 spring onion, finely shredded

Lightly cooked broccoli

Melt the honey, orange zest and juice in a small saucepan over a moderate heat and simmer till syrupy, adding the lime juice a few seconds before removing the pan from the heat. Set aside.

Heat a non-stick pan or griddle pan. Preheat the oven to 160°C.

Slice the pork into 6 even sized pieces, only brush with the olive oil if your pan is not non-stick, season with salt and pepper. Sear in the hot pan for 3 minutes on each side until well browned, then turn onto their round sides to brown for a minute or two, turning to finish the searing. Transfer to a warm serving dish in the oven, while you cook the plums.

Brush the plums with a little of the honey syrup then fry (on a lower heat than the pork), cut side down for 3 minutes, then turn to cook for 2 or 3 minutes more. Splash a little water in the pan if the plums are cooking too quickly, you want them to be soft and juicy, not burned. Transfer to the dish with the pork and keep warm while you warm the honey sauce and cook the broccoli.

Divide the pork and plums between two warm plates, spoon over a little of the sauce, sprinkle with some of the shredded spring onion and serve with the broccoli.

SLOW ROAST BELLY PORK

You will need

2kg piece Specially Selected Pork belly, the rind deeply scored (ask for the end with fewer bones, to make carving easier)

2tsp salt

For the paste

2 cloves garlic, peeled

1tsp salt

½ tsp freshly ground black pepper

2tsp fennel seeds (or dried rosemary)

Preheat the oven to 220°C.

Crush all the ingredients for the paste together in a mortar and pestle if you have one, or with the end of a rolling-pin if not.

Place the pork skin side down on a board and trim away any excess fat from the underside. With a sharp knife slash the flesh quite lightly in a criss-cross pattern. Rub the garlic paste well into the cuts and all over the meat's surface.

Turn the belly pork skin side up again on the board and rub the salt well into the skin, making sure it comes into contact with the fat layer to ensure good crisp crackling.

Place the pork on a wire rack within a large roasting tin to allow for the fat to run away from the meat during the slow cooking process. Roast in the hot oven for 30 minutes to get the crackling going and then reduce the oven temperature to 160°C for a further 2½ – 3 hours when much of the fat will have drained away, leaving a lovely crisp topped juicy piece of meat.

Delicious hot or cold.

ONE POT WONDER

You will need

2kg Specially Selected Pork leg or shoulder meat, diced into 2½cm pieces

3tbsp olive oil

15g butter

500g shallots, peeled and left whole

300g small whole carrots, scrubbed and trimmed

3 sticks celery cut into 4cm lengths

200g button mushrooms, wiped

3 sprigs thyme

150ml white wine

750g pork or chicken stock

3tbsp plain flour, seasoned with salt and pepper

Preheat the oven to 170°C.

In a deep frying pan gently fry the shallots with 1tbsp of olive oil and the butter for about 10 minutes until well browned and beginning to soften, then add the carrots and continue cooking for 2 or 3 minutes more. Transfer to a large casserole dish. In the oil remaining in the frying pan lightly brown the mushrooms and soften the celery, remove to a separate dish, set aside till later.

Toss the meat in the seasoned flour and fry in batches in the remaining olive oil until well browned on all sides, transfer the meat to the casserole.

Pour the wine into the frying pan and heat, stirring, to gather up all the lovely flavoursome sticky bits from the base of the pan, add the stock and bring to the boil.

Tuck the thyme sprigs into the casserole, pour the stock mixture over the meat and stir well. Cover with the lid and put into the oven for one hour and 45 minutes.

After this time add the celery and mushrooms to the pot, stir carefully and check the seasoning. Return to the oven for about 45 minutes or until the meat is nice and tender.

Lovely served with mashed potato; or a mix of mashed root vegetables such as potatoes, parsnips and sweet potatoes or celeriac.

RED THAI PORK

with noodles

You will need

225g lean Specially Selected Pork fillet, cut into thin slices

5ml oil

30ml red Thai curry paste

3 spring onions, sliced

50g sugar snap peas

1 red pepper, deseeded and sliced

1 red chilli, deseeded and sliced

2 heads pak choi, sliced

150ml coconut milk

1tbsp fresh coriander, chopped

For the noodles:

100g dried rice or egg noodles

Juice of 1 lime

15ml sweet chilli sauce

Fresh coriander, chopped, to garnish

1 spring onion, sliced

In a large non-stick wok or pan, fry the pork in oil until browned. Stir through red Thai curry paste and add spring onions, sugar snap peas, red pepper, red chilli and pak choi. Cook for 2 – 3 minutes.

Add the coconut milk and heat for 1 – 2 minutes until sauce has thickened slightly. Sprinkle with fresh chopped coriander.

For the noodles, cook the rice or noodles according to pack instructions. Drain and stir through the lime juice, sweet chilli sauce, fresh chopped coriander and spring onion.

Serve the stir-fry with the noodles.

HOMEMADE MEATBALLS

You will need

450g Specially Selected Pork mince
1 small onion, finely chopped
2tbsp fresh breadcrumbs
2tbsp cream
1 egg yolk
1tbsp parsley or chives, finely chopped
Salt and pepper
2tbsp olive oil

For the tomato sauce

750g large ripe tomatoes, skinned and coarsely chopped
1 large onion, peeled and finely chopped

2 cloves garlic, crushed
2tbsp olive oil
100ml red wine
100ml water
2tsp oregano, chopped
Salt and pepper
500g fresh pappardelle (or 300g if dried)
1tbsp flat leaf parsley, finely chopped
A little olive oil
A chunk of fresh parmesan to grate
1tsp sugar (optional)

In a large bowl mix together all the meatball ingredients except the oil, then with wet hands, roll the mixture into walnut sized balls. Set aside to chill while you prepare the sauce.

Heat a large deep sauté pan over a low heat and fry the onions and garlic in the oil until soft and just beginning to brown (6 minutes). Add the tomatoes and oregano, stir, then cook a minute more before adding the wine and water. Bring to the boil and reduce the heat and simmer gently for about 15 minutes until thick and pulpy. Add a little more water if necessary, then season with salt and pepper and if the sauce is a little sour, add some sugar and taste again until just right for you!

While the sauce is simmering fry the meatballs in the oil until brown all over, do this in batches if the pan is not big enough, then remove to a plate with a slotted spoon. Once the sauce is ready add the meat balls to it and stir gently to coat them and simmer very gently (about 10 minutes) until cooked through but still a little soft.

Bring a large pot of water to the boil and cook the pasta according to the pack instructions then drain and divide between four warm plates. Dress with a little olive oil and parsley and top with some meatballs, plenty of sauce and grated parmesan.

SERVES
6

PREPARATION
20 mins

COOKING
2 hrs **40** mins

ROLLED STUFFED SHOULDER OF PORK

You will need

2kg Specially Selected Pork shoulder, boned and skin deeply scored

Salt and pepper

For the stuffing

1 medium leek, washed and thinly sliced

1tbsp olive oil or butter

1 stick celery, finely chopped

150g white breadcrumbs (made from day-old bread that has lost some of its moisture)

75g walnuts, chopped

60g raisins or sultanas, soaked in the juice of a small orange

2tbsp fresh sage, finely chopped (or 2tsp dried sage)

Handful fresh parsley, chopped

A little milk to bind, if needed

For the roast potatoes

1kg floury potatoes, peeled and cut into large chunks, par-boiled for 7 or 8 minutes in lightly salted boiling water, then drained

For the gravy

100ml white wine or cider

300ml pork or chicken stock

100ml water

1tbsp Dijon mustard

Preheat the oven to 220°C.

Gently sauté the leek in the oil or butter for about 5 minutes until softened and transparent, add the celery and cook for a further 2 minutes. Mix with all the rest of the stuffing ingredients, except the milk which you will only need to add if the stuffing seems too crumbly. Moisten with a little milk if necessary. Season to taste with salt and pepper.

Continued over...

Open out the boned meat, skin side down and spoon the stuffing onto the meat. Roll up neatly but not too tightly, so the stuffing won't be squeezed out during cooking. Secure with skewers or tie at intervals with string. To stop the cut, stuffed sides of the meat from over browning, place a double layer of baking parchment or oiled foil over the stuffing and secure with cocktail sticks.

Place the meat in a roasting tin, joint facing down, pat the skin dry with kitchen paper then rub all over with salt and pepper making sure it gets into contact with the fat layer in order to make good crackling.

Roast in the hot oven for about 30 minutes before reducing the heat to 170°C, continue cooking for another 2 hours or so until cooked to your liking. Add the par-boiled potatoes to the meat tin for the last hour of cooking, turning occasionally. Transfer the pork and potatoes to a warm serving dish, cover with foil, allow the meat to rest while you make the gravy.

Pour off any excess fat from the pan, add the wine and the stock and stir up all the sticky bits from the base of the pan, add the water. Heat to just below boiling point and reduce the liquid by half, add the mustard to thicken the gravy and check the seasoning

Serve the meat cut into thickish slices, making sure everyone gets some stuffing, with vegetables and a spoonful of gravy.

STEP BY STEP

BROWNING CUBED STEAK FOR CASSEROLES

Trim any fat from the steak.

Separate the main pieces along the seams of fat.

Cut into bite sized cubes.

Put flour (1tbsp per kilo of meat) in a bowl, add salt and pepper and mix together.

Browning cubed steak for casseroles

Add the beef cubes in batches to the seasoned flour, turn until all the meat is coated.

Heat oil in a large pan and add the floured beef in small batches to the pan.

Turn the beef to brown all over.

Remove from the pan and add the remaining batches until all browned.

Carving a leg of lamb

I.

Remove from the oven and rest for 10 – 15 minutes.

2.

Position the joint, steadying it with a large fork.

STEP BY STEP

Cut a wedge shaped slice from the middle.

Continue to cut slices until you reach the socket bone.

CARVING A LEG OF LAMB

Once the small socket bone is reached, carefully cut around.

Continue to slice.

STEP BY STEP

7.

Turn the bone in your hand and carefully slice the meat off.

8.

Continue slicing until it is virtually meat free.

Preparing pork for perfect crackling

Make sure the pork is completely dry.

Using a very sharp knife score the pork rind.

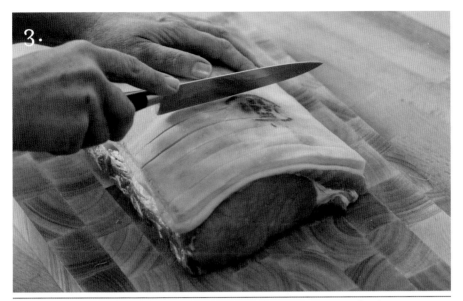

Use vertical lines about a finger width apart – taking care not to cut too far down.

Turn the pork skin side down.

PREPARING PORK FOR PERFECT CRACKLING

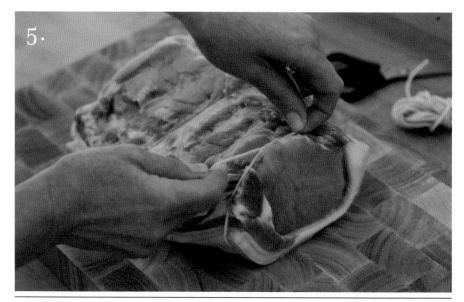

Starting at the end tie with string across the joint.

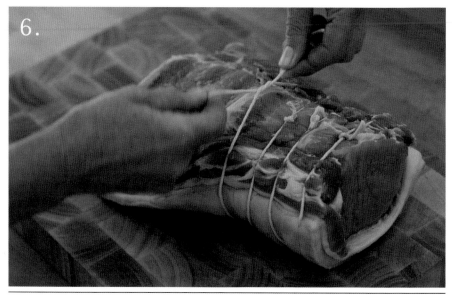

Repeat this process across the joint to the other end.

STEP BY STEP

Sit the pork in a baking tray and rub the skin with sea salt.

Roast the pork uncovered.

Nutrition

Recipe	Kcals	Fat (g)	Protein (g)	Carbohydrates (g)	Sugar (g)	Salt (g)
BEEF						
Beef stir fry	535	16.7	33.7	62.5	6.5	1.5
Roast rib of beef	518	22.4	67.2	11.5	10.3	1.7
Fillet of beef	315	18.0	34.8	3.5	0.6	1.4
Beef satay	229	8.6	38.1	24.9	3.2	0.8
Easy Asian noodle soup	223	6.0	16.4	26.2	4.3	1.5
Szechuan style orange beef	434	22.4	35.7	22.5	17.3	0.8
Rather special beef burger	587	25.8	42.5	49.4	8.3	1.7
Beef carpaccio tartlets	611	35.8	31.9	39.8	3.7	1.3
LAMB						
Mustard & herb crusted lamb	661	55.3	29.7	11.9	3.7	0.3
Rolled lamb shoulder	411	22.4	37.2	16.2	5.4	1.4
Lamb chump roast	299	20.5	23.3	0.1	4.9	0.7
Slow cooked lamb	681	44.4	41.7	30.4	4.6	0.8
Lamb moussaka	413	23.3	37.1	16.2	9.6	1.0
Griddled lamb steaks	424	21.8	49.5	7.8	7.1	2.7
Spicy lamb curry	368	26.0	19.7	15.5	9.9	0.5
Lamb en croûte	583	39.0	25.5	34.5	1.3	1.2
PORK						
Skewered pork fillet	297	12.9	38.5	6.9	5.8	0.7
Pork chops	449	19.7	65.1	3.1	2.2	1.9
Pan-fried pork medallions	254	8.2	25.9	18.9	16.3	1.2
Slow roast belly pork	733	53.5	62.9	0.1	0.0	2.4
One pot wonder	389	11.8	56.9	11.4	5.1	1.0
Red Thai pork	464	14.6	35.5	50.5	14.4	2.5
Homemade meatballs	741	27.1	39.4	80.4	12.9	0.9
Rolled stuffed shoulder of pork	774	30.7	83.8	38.7	6.8	1.5